EVANGELIZING CHILDREN

Published by: Discipleship Ministries of the Mesoamerica Region
www.discipleship.MesoamericaRegion.org
www.SdmiResources.MesoamericaRegion.org

Translated from Spanish and edited by Monte Cyr

ISBN: 978-1-63580-190-3

Developed by *Rafael Serrano*
Spanish Editor: *Patricia Picavea*
Spanish Coeditor: *Mery Asenjo*
Design and layout: *Slater Designer / Slater Joel Chavez*
Cover photography: *<a href="https://www.freepik.es/fotos-vectores-gratis/ninos">Foto de Niños
creado por freepik - www.freepik.es</a>*

Printed in the United States

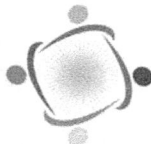

Mesoamerica Region

CONTENTS

Introduction :: 4

1. The Importance of Evangelizing Children ::::::::::::::::: 6

2. Characteristics of Evangelism to Children :::::::::::::: 10

3. Characteristics of the Leader Who Works With Children :: 17

4. Evangelism Strategies for Children :::::::::::::::::::::::::: 24

5. After Evangelism: Discipling Children :::::::::::::::::::: 42

Bonus, Plan of Salvation :: 50

INTRODUCTION

We can never doubt the productive work of evangelists in leading people to Jesus Christ. However, it is good to note that there is a series of actions prior to the evangelistic event that prepare the way, such as intercessory prayer for a person, an invitation, counsel, a good testimony, etc. These forms of preparation have been passed on from one generation to another until reaching our time, helping Christianity to spread more and more.

We believe that the noble task of evangelizing is more fruitful if we take into account the above, and also, if we work as a church to achieve it. This Evangelizing Children manual gives some suggestions to help you in this great work for children.

Likewise, it is known to all of us that the results of evangelistic work do not only lie in human action, for the best evangelistic methods will be useless if we neglect the indispensable intervention and direction of the Holy Spirit. Let us bear in mind that evangelization is not simply proselytizing, because if we wanted such a thing, we would be no better than the Pharisees. The evangelization of children is about presenting boys and girls to Christ, the person who can transform their lives.

The main purpose of evangelism is to help the child and his or her family, so that their conditions of life change through the regenerative power of Jesus Christ, which will bring growth in the church as an addition.

For some time, there has been a noticeable awakening among Christians regarding the importance of evangelization. The church is the medium that the Lord Jesus Christ chose to accomplish this task. That is why we must unite and work toward the objective that this evangelistic mission is fulfilled.

Through evangelization and the proclamation of the love of Jesus Christ, the Son of God, as the only one who offers human beings salvation and eternal life, true change will be seen in the lives of children. We must bear in mind that the gospel is "the power of God that brings salvation to everyone who believes ..." (Romans 1:16).

This evangelism manual is the fruit of experience and hard work with children. Its objective is to facilitate the work of all those interested in the evangelization of boys and girls. We hope that everything shared will be of great help to those who feel motivated to assume this responsibility that will be a great blessing for the church of Christ.

"Start children off on the way they should go, and even when they are old they will not turn from it."
(Proverbs 22:6)

01 The Importance of Evangelizing Children

There are three very important reasons to evangelize children:

a. Boys and girls, like adults, are lost. Their hearts are polluted by sin, and their path is the way of death. Therefore, they need to be found. The Bible says, *"all have sinned, and fall short of the glory of God"* (Romans 3:23).

b. Christ taught that children are important: *"whoever takes the lowly position of this child is the greatest in the kingdom of heaven. And whoever welcomes one such child in my name welcomes me"* (Matthew 18:4-5).

c. Because childhood is a precious stage in which sufficient humility is manifested to know God's love and believe with faith. The Word says: *"At that time the disciples came to Jesus and asked, 'Who, then, is the greatest in the kingdom of heaven?' He called a little child to him, and placed the child among them. And he said: 'Truly I tell you, unless you change and become like little children, you will never enter the kingdom of heaven'"* (Matthew 18: 1-3).

A. Children are important to God

Jesus loves boys and girls; they are very important people to Him. According to Mark 10:13-16, the Master did not reject them; rather, he drew them to himself, and laying his hands on them, he blessed them.

For some people, out of the mouths of boys and girls only come sounds without reason, phrases without meaning, or ideas without importance. However, this is not so. The spirit of each one of them is open and accessible to the voice of God, making it possible to communicate with Him. Remember that the Bible says that the Lord listens to everyone who calls on Him (Jeremiah 29: 12-13).

We must learn from this sensitivity that boys and girls have so that God can reveal even more things to us. They do not ask questions just to satisfy reason or knowledge of their mind alone. Rather, they are curious about what they feel: their emotions, their desires or their relationships with others and with their environment. Because of all of this, it is children who are most likely to openly receive the Word of the Lord.

They focus on the most important or primary thing, which is joy and happiness, and not upon the material, rational or economic. Children think and believe that what the Word of God says and promises is true. Their belief or faith is not limited; rather it is natural and real (Luke 10:21).

B. The importance of evangelizing children

Every person can be evangelized from an early age, even if we think that there is an age of responsibility, that is, when good and evil can be known in a broader way. Many people place that age at between five and eleven years old. However, this cannot be a hard and fast rule, for some people testify to having known the Lord long before the early part of the age range mentioned.

So who can categorically say that there is a specific age, and not before, at which it is possible to make a responsible decision for Christ? It is vitally important that the gospel is presented to children at an early age. However, we must be careful, because at this age, many times boys or girls respond to an altar call, or pray to accept Christ, because other children are doing it, without understanding what they are really doing. Therefore, we must be careful and make the call on special occasions such as during children's evangelistic campaigns, or in times when we see that boys and girls are sensitive to the message of salvation, without falling into something repetitive that over time they can ignore.

All God requires to save us is simple faith. He will look at each person according to their knowledge and ability. For those who are four years old, God will be satisfied with a four-year old response of faith. For those who are eight years old, God will accept a faith of that age, etc. Whether they are a boy or a girl, God will gladly receive their simple childlike faith.

With early salvation, early growth in grace is also experienced. The Christian life is a process that, the earlier you start, the greater the growth that is possible. The statistics interestingly show us the following:

Converted between
15 and 30 years old

Converted after 30
years of age

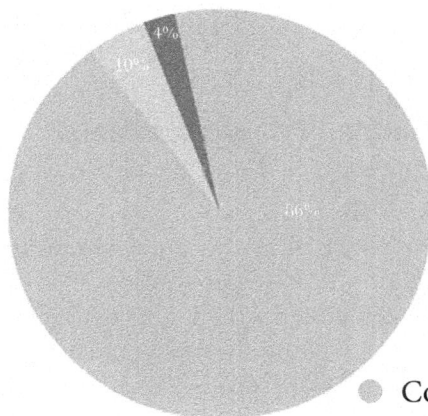

Converted before
15 years of age

In this graph, it can be seen that 86% of the believers interviewed indicated that they made their faith decision before the age of 15. This tells us of the importance of taking advantage of that valuable and precious stage of childhood in which, as already mentioned, a person has the necessary humility and sincere faith to know God.

To conclude this first chapter, evangelism to children is urgent. There are growing pressures faced by the new generations, and new ideologies are trying to reach them. In addition, today we notice a large number of disintegrated and unstable homes, which makes the lives of many children increasingly difficult. But we, the church of Christ, have the message of salvation in Christ Jesus, which must be urgently communicated to all children. It can change their lives and help them overcome the various difficult circumstances that come their way.

02 Characteristics of Evangelism to Children

A. Where can children be evangelized?

Any place where the Holy Spirit guides us to evangelize can be good. If the child is from a Christian home, the natural place may be at their home with their parents and siblings, or at the church where they attend. Parents can be the best guides for their sons and daughters since in their hearts lie the interest, love, patience, information and the ability to begin to instruct them in the Christian walk, and all this from the example of their lives.

Many times, God speaks to boys and girls during worship services generally directed to adults, in which invitations are made to the altar. The boys and girls understand the message, and decide to move forward in search of salvation. Altar counselors, or local children's ministry leaders, should be on the lookout for this in order to approach and ask them why they have come to the altar, and thus give them the appropriate counsel.

There are also activities or events that are specific for evangelizing children. These can be done in the park, in schools, in homes, and anywhere the opportunity to talk about Jesus presents itself. Also, and mainly, the Sunday school class is a great time to evangelize boys and girls. These are fertile grounds to receive the seed of the gospel. So if the teachers are attentive and aware of their students, they will be able to be used by the Lord to make good use of the opportunities that come their way.

B. Who can evangelize children?

One of the requirements to evangelize boys and girls is that personal communication and trust must be established with them.

Another important aspect is to know the scriptures well; that is, be familiar with the biblical passages that are evangelistic, using simple vocabulary so that the message of salvation in Jesus Christ can be easily understood. An equally important aspect is having a love for evangelism ... especially for children.

Sunday school teachers and family members of boys and girls, by their position or relationship with them, are naturally suitable instruments to bring them closer to Christ. Each week, in each meeting or class, there is a natural interaction so that you can get to know them very well. For this reason, local church children's ministry leaders and parents must be sensitive to the spiritual needs of their little ones.

Although there are people who work specifically with children such as Sunday school teachers, evangelists, disciplers, Christian clowns, etc. in special circumstances, any person mature in their faith can lead a boy or a girl to Christ, since this responsibility belongs to all believers.

C. How do I guide a child to Christ?

At this point, the steps to follow to guide children to Christ, the considerations necessary to do so effectively, and other important points will be presented.

1. Knowing the necessary scriptures

As already indicated above, it is necessary that the person who evangelizes knows the Scriptures well. At a minimum, there is a set of verses that you need to study beforehand in order to know well the redemptive plan of God, and to present the message of the gospel of Christ Jesus in a simple way. We recommend marking these verses in your Bible with a special color, and spend considerable time praying and studying the biblical passages which are presented below.

Who needs to be saved?

(1) "There is no one righteous, not even one;" (Romans 3:10).

(2) "for all have sinned and fall short of the glory of God," (Romans 3:23).

Who can save?

(1) "Look, the Lamb of God, who takes away the sin of the world!" (John 1:29).

(2) "Here is a trustworthy saying that deserves full acceptance: Christ Jesus came into the world to save sinners…" (1 Timothy 1:15).

How Christ saves?

(1) "For God so loved the world that he gave his one and only Son, that whoever believes in him shall not perish but have eternal life." (John 3:16).

(2) "But God demonstrates his own love for us in this: While we were still sinners, Christ died for us." (Romans 5:8).

(3) "He himself bore our sins" in his body on the cross, so that we might die to sins and live for righteousness; "by his wounds you have been healed." (1 Peter 2:24).

What must we do to be saved?

(1) "Yet to all who did receive him, to those who believed in his name, he gave the right to become children of God" (John 1:12).

(2) "Believe in the Lord Jesus, and you will be saved—you and your household" (Acts 16:31).

What happens when we trust in Jesus?

(1) "So if the Son sets you free, you will be free indeed." (John 8:36).

(2) "Therefore, if anyone is in Christ, the new creation has come: The old has gone, the new is here!" (2 Corinthians 5:17).

What do we do after we receive the gift of salvation?

(1) "Commit your way to the Lord; trust in him and he will do this" (Psalm 37:5).

(2) "And whatever you do, whether in word or deed, do it all in the name of the Lord Jesus, giving thanks to God the Father through him" (Colossians 3:17).

What is our obligation to other people?

(1) "But you will receive power when the Holy Spirit comes on you; and you will be my witnesses in Jerusalem, and in all Judea and Samaria, and to the ends of the earth" (Acts 1:8).

(2) "while we wait for the blessed hope—the appearing of the glory of our great God and Savior, Jesus Christ" (Titus 2:13).

2. Considerations when making the invitation

When presenting the gospel message, consider these valuable recommendations:

a. Be sensitive to the leading of the Holy Spirit. He is the only one who can convince someone of their need for the Savior (John 16: 7-8). Therefore, do not try to create a sense of guilt in children.

b. Have a plan of action. Plan with the children's ministry team what you will do when boys and girls respond to the invitation. If possible, prepare at least one helper to work with those children who do not respond affirmatively to the invitation while you pray with those who do accept the Lord Jesus.

c. Use words or expressions that are understandable to children. For example, if you use the word "sin," explain that sins are "bad things or bad actions" that we have done, and give examples of this (lying, cheating on a test, disobeying parents, etc.).

d. **Allow time for the Holy Spirit to speak to the boys and girls.** It is not our human words that speak to them, but God through his Spirit. So trust Him. Also, keep in mind not to extend the invitation too long if no child responds affirmatively.

3. Biblical rationale for making the invitation

There are many biblical quotes that we can use to make the invitation and show the steps to follow to receive Christ as their Savior. One of those biblical quotes is John 3:16. The following is a brief explanation that can be used to introduce the plan of salvation to children.

John 3:16	Brief explanation for the children
"For God so loved the world"	This means that God loves you, me, him, her, etc. This means that God loves all people.
"that he gave his one and only Son"	God sent his son Jesus from heaven to come here to earth.
"that whoever believes in him"	This refers to any person who sincerely believes that Jesus came into the world, died, and rose again for their salvation. And you can be one of those people.
"shall not perish"	In other words, if you believe in Jesus and ask for forgiveness for the bad things you have done; God will not punish you.
"but have eternal life."	his means that after you die, you will go to live in heaven forever with God.

The eyes of the boy's or girl's heart should be directed to our Lord Jesus Christ as Savior and Lord. Only in Him is there eternal life (John 14:6). It is not enough to describe the greatness of the Lord's sacrifice;

rather, it must be emphasized that He died for each person. In this part, it is suggested to approach the matter as something personal, directed to each child. In other words, they must be told that Jesus Christ paid the punishment they deserved for the bad things they did (sins).

4. How to help boys and girls pray and understand their prayer

When a boy or a girl has understood the message of salvation and wishes to pray to accept Jesus as their Savior, we suggest the following:

a. If possible, talk individually with each boy and girl.

b. Let each one tell you why they want to pray. He or she may or may not be seeking salvation. Rather, they may want to pray for a sick friend or family member. If the child does not express a spiritual need, pray briefly for him or her and the request they are sharing with you.

c. Use scriptures to personalize the invitation. We suggest you read John 3:16 and 1 John 1: 9 to them, inserting the name of the boy or girl. If he or she expresses a spiritual need, present the plan of salvation. Once this has been explained, lead them in a time of prayer with the Lord. This can be done by explaining that it is similar to inviting a person or family member who he or she appreciates into their home. So if they want the Lord Jesus to enter their heart, they need to tell him that and invite him in and say: "Jesus, please come into my heart. Come into my life. I accept you as my Savior." It is important that the child say the following in their own words, and with the greatest possible understanding and conviction:

- Ask God for forgiveness for the wrong things they have done, telling him that they regret all of those things.

- Believe that Jesus Christ died for the wrong things they have done, and trust Jesus to be their Savior.

In this part, we suggest that you, as a children's leader, not use the word "sin." Rather, explain this word/concept with practical examples, such as lies, theft, acting mean, etc., as we mentioned earlier.

d. Allow the child to pray. If he or she hesitates, say something like this: "Tell God that you know that you have done wrong. Ask Him to forgive you. And also tell Him that you believe that Jesus died for your sins and that you want to live like He wants you to live."

When they finish praying, ask, "What has God done for you?" Avoid using leading questions such as, "Has Jesus saved you yet?" Let the child tell you what has happened. If they say that they prayed, but don't know if God forgave them, explain that the Lord forgave them even if they feel nothing. That is faith!

If the child is not sure, the procedure may need to be repeated, taking time to explain each step when appropriate. Also consider as a possibility that the child is not ready yet. If this is the case, don't pressure them because they may do what you ask then to do in order to be accepted or impress you.

Whenever you pray for a boy or a girl, thank God for loving them, no matter what decision they made. And if they accepted the Lord Jesus, pray that God will help them grow in Him.

Likewise, it may be the case that the boy or girl knows about their sin, and has asked for salvation that is in Christ, but has never felt that it was real in their life. John 1:12 says: "Yet to all who did receive him, to those who believed in his name, he gave the right to become children of God." This can help them with this. Believing is receiving, and receiving is believing. That is, to believe, there must be a voluntary reception of Christ. The child must say (at least inwardly): "Come into my heart, Lord Jesus," and feel that they need the Lord. They need to say something that expresses and indicates their voluntary acceptance of Jesus, from their heart. If they do that, God's Word promises them that they are now forgiven, they are God's child, and they are now part of the family of God.

03 Characteristics of the Leader who Works with Children

All of God's servants are exposed to the eyes of others, and many follow our footsteps very closely. As leaders, we are in a window that everyone can see. There are boys and girls who want to be like their leader because this is their closest example of what it looks like to follow Jesus. Therefore, it is important that everyone who wants to work with children be a Christian of good testimony and firm convictions. Next, we will deal with various aspects related to this point.

A. Moral Issues

Although the subject of sex is a matter that is not always easy to deal with, we must mention what the 2017-2021 Manual of our Church of the Nazarene says in the Appendix, chapter IV (Current Moral and Social Issues), in section 916, where it talks about the mistreatment of the defenseless:

The Church of the Nazarene abhors abuse of any person of any age or sex and calls for increased public awareness through its publications and by providing appropriate educational information.

The Church of the Nazarene reaffirms its historical policy that all those who act under the authority of the Church are prohibited from sexual misconduct and other forms of abuse of the unempowered. When placing people in positions of trust or authority, the Church of the Nazarene will presume that past conduct is usually a reliable indicator of likely future behavior. The Church

will withhold positions of authority from people who have previously used a position of trust or authority to engage in sexual misconduct or abuse of the unempowered, unless appropriate steps are taken to prevent future wrongful behavior. Expressions of remorse by a guilty person shall not be considered sufficient to overcome the presumption that future wrongful conduct is likely, unless the expressions of remorse are accompanied by an observable change of conduct for a sufficient length of time, to indicate that a repeat of the wrongful misconduct is unlikely. (2009)

Manual Church of the Nazarene, 2017-2021. p.393-394

The church is not exempt from having troublesome people among its membership and friends who will want to take advantage of the innocence of children. Thus, we strongly recommend that when choosing the leaders who will work with them, that choice be made only after a thorough evaluation. We want to urge leaders who work with children to be extremely careful in dealing with children. Children place all their trust in adults and respect authority without question. For this reason, we offer the following suggestions:

1. To develop the leadership of people who are role models for children, it is recommended that where possible, both women and men work in the team that make up the Children's Ministry.

2. As a leader, be observant of the conduct of your fellow leaders, and report any abnormality you observe to the pastor or senior leader. Be careful and use good judgment; do not comment or start unfounded rumors (Leviticus 19:16; Psalm 101:5; 1 Timothy 5:13).

3. Plan activities so that there is always more than one adult with the participating children.

4. When a child expresses that a leader has kissed, touched, or caressed him or her incorrectly, believe what he or she is telling you and immediately speak with the ministry director and / or the pastor. Never share the matter with other people. Act in the same way if a child reports abusive behavior on the part of their parents or relatives.

5. If children need to be helped to go to the toilet, it is recommended that a woman take the girls and a man take the boys.

6. The person accompanying the child must notify another adult where he/she will be, and should return with the child to the activity room as soon as possible.

With these rules, we do not want to create mistrust towards leaders. We just want to give guidelines to apply to everyone equally. In this way, there will be no room for bad situations.

We are a holiness church, and we must not let anything damage our image, since that would damage the image of Christ. If secular entities take great care with children, how much more should we, as the Lord's church.

(You can download a more extensive child safety policy at: *http://www.mesoamericaregion.org/en/package/child-protection-policy/*)

B. The leader of children must be a disciple of the Lord

The leader needs to be a disciple of Christ so that He can perfect him/her day by day. In this way, they will be a good visible role model for the children and be able to show the Teacher of teachers with their life. Luke 6:40 says, "The student is not above the teacher, but everyone who is fully trained will be like their teacher."

It doesn't matter how young the leader is. They should be an example to all believers. The fact that he or she is young is no excuse for not being a good witness in their Christian life. Let us remember the instruction that the Apostle Paul gave to Timothy, a young leader: "Don't let anyone look down on you because you are young, but set an example for the believers in speech, in conduct, in love, in faith and in purity" (1 Timothy 4:12).

Likewise, it is important that the leader does not have feelings of superiority with respect to other people. On the contrary, the leader must be grateful for the mercy of God, and for the blessing of being able to serve him and be His instrument. In conclusion, the leader must be filled with the Holy Spirit so that God ministers through him or her.

Anyone who wishes to dedicate themself to this fruitful ministry of evangelism to children must seriously prepare themself. They should never think that this is a trivial ministry. Their preparation must begin in their heart. The person must be completely sure of their own salvation by grace, through faith. They must daily seek a clean heart through confession of wrongdoing. And if the Lord helps them see that they sinned in something, they must repent immediately and genuinely. Our God is holy; and we, his sons and daughters, have been called to holiness (1 Peter 1:15).

Likewise, the leader must believe with all certainty in the salvation of boys and girls, and continually ask God to give them a feeling of concern, coming from heaven, towards the little sheep for whom Christ died, so that they may soon be led to the flock of the Good Shepherd.

C. Profile of the leader who works with children

The following are the main general characteristics of the character and / or personality of the leader who works with children:

1. Has experienced full conversion and is living a life of holiness.

2. Has a spirit of service and dedication to the Lord's work among children.

3. Craves to present the gospel of the kingdom of God to children.

4. Has sensitivity, patience and empathy in dealing with boys and girls.

5. Has a stable and mature personality, adaptable to circumstances.

6. Has a high degree of perseverance in working with children.

7. Is perceptive in detecting the spiritual, emotional, physical, or material needs of boys and girls.

8. Has the ability to establish and maintain strong interpersonal relationships.

9. Has good grooming.

D. Devotional life of the leader working with children

1. **Personal conversion experience.** The proclamation of the gospel has as its primary objective the conversion of people to a new life in Christ Jesus. From this we can affirm that no person will be able to evangelize another if they have not first experienced in their own life what an authentic conversion is.

2. **Constant search for a life filled with the Holy Spirit.** When you have the Holy Spirit, you feel secure, confident, and feel the need to speak the Word of God to all people. Let us not forget that our Lord Jesus said: "But you will receive power when the Holy Spirit comes on you; and you will be my witnesses in Jerusalem, and in all Judea and Samaria, and to the ends of the earth." (Acts 1: 8)

3. **Prayer and fasting.** These spiritual disciplines are powerful instruments for successful ministry, and specifically in our case, for evangelizing and discipling boys and girls (Acts 13:2-3).

4. **Prior knowledge and study of the Bible.** No one can give what they do not have. So effective evangelism requires a reasoned knowledge of the Scriptures. Think about this: how can someone preach/teach/communicate the gospel if they have not first understood it in the light of God's Word? Hence the importance of searching the Bible, knowing it, and then transmitting it faithfully (1 Peter 3:15). As something complementary, it is good that we review the concepts written in Ephesians 6:10-20. We must be prepared when Satan launches his attacks (v.13).

E. The leader who works with children should avoid:

1. Stopping praying and studying the Bible.

2. Allowing anger to take possession of them.

3. Being late for scheduled activities.

4. Ridiculing the faith of boys and girls.

5. Prolonging the talk too long when presenting the gospel, or trying to convince children by relying on their own human efforts.

6. Getting into arguments.

7. Getting discouraged if they "don't succeed" when they present the gospel message. It is God's work, and we are his instruments. If there are not any boys or girls who decide to receive Jesus Christ as their Savior and Lord, the leader shouldn't get discouraged. That doesn't mean their efforts were in vain. They need to move on.

8. Giving place to vain comments.

9. Stopping attending scheduled activities without communicating in advance.

F. **The leader who works with children should always seek to:**

1. Find out about the context in which the evangelistic message will be presented (reality of childhood, the needs, place where the event will take place, resources that will be available, etc.).

2. Recognize and accept the limitations that will arise.

3. Prepare the evangelistic message in advance.

4. Bring the materials they will need to present the message from God's Word.

5. Always carry their Bible.

6. Always respond to boys and girls with love, and demonstrate it at all times through their attitude and positive vocabulary.

7. Bring evangelistic brochures or materials appropriate for the ages of the boys and girls.

8. Show their enthusiasm for God's Word.

9. Listen carefully to the children.

10. Thank them for their attention and say goodbye politely.

G. **The training of the leader who works with children**

It is undeniable that God is the one who calls people to work with children. He puts in people's hearts a fervent desire to serve him in this area. Linked to this is the leader's responsibility to train according to their possibilities. Our denomination and other ecclesiastical and non-ecclesiastical institutions offer various face-to-face and / or virtual training programs for leaders who work with children, providing them with tools and knowledge for their ministry. To effectively take advantage of this, it is advised that the leader, with the guidance of other more experienced leaders, use these resources and others to train regularly.

04 Evangelism Strategies for Children

A. In Sunday school, cell groups, or Bible study

Sunday school classes, cell groups, or Bible studies are special times for evangelism because the leader is with the boys and girls every week. For this reason, it is good to consider the following suggestions:

1. Make a list with the personal data of the boys and girls who have already accepted Christ as their Savior and Lord.

2. Prepare another list with the personal data of new contacts of boys and girls who can be invited on special occasions (celebration of Children's Day, Christmas, etc.).

3. Establish a special relationship with the boys and girls. This will help you know their spiritual situations and needs, enabling you to help them when they need it.

4. Organize evangelistic services for children, where children and teachers collaborate.

5. Teach biblical doctrine to boys and girls. This will prepare their hearts to receive the seed of the gospel.

6. Train boys and girls in personal evangelism.

B. Personal Evangelism

Personal evangelism is one of the most dynamic forms of sharing the gospel. For this reason, the evangelistic method to be used must be applied in a very creative way, and must have the following characteristics:

1. **Interesting:** you have to get and hold their attention right away.

2. **Simple:** You have to present the gospel at the level of the child's understanding.

3. **Short:** you have to present the entire plan of salvation in two to five minutes. It is very important to put into practice the Rule of 1 x 1 (one minute of lesson / preaching per child's year of age).

4. **Visualized** (illustrated): it has to appeal to several of the five senses, especially sight and hearing. Thus, consideration should be given to using colors and images that visually communicate the gospel to children.

5. **Active:** it must motivate the full and continuous participation of the boy or girl throughout the presentation.

6. **Planned, organized and prepared:** it must be biblical and complete; that is, it has to include two elements:

   • A child's invitation to another child (the Big Brother Plan, each boy and girl praying and inviting their peers)

   • An immediate follow-up plan for the discipleship of newly converted boys and girls.

C. Evangelistic Methods for Personal Evangelism

Here are some examples of personal evangelistic methods for someone to share the gospel with a boy or girl. It is suggested to teach these methods to the boys and girls of the church so that they too can evangelize other children by making early use of the abilities that the Lord has given them.

1. "The eye exam"

Materials:

- Visual aids: five cards of different colors with drawings or illustrations, and a word or phrase.
  - ◊ *Green* (with drawings of the world, word - ***creation***)
  - ◊ *Dark Gray* (with a dirty or stained heart that cannot enter heaven, word - ***sin***. You can also have words that describe sin, like lying, cheating, stealing, etc.)
  - ◊ *Red* (with an illustration of the cross representing the death of Jesus; word - ***Jesus***)
  - ◊ *White* (with a clean heart, after the person asks God for forgiveness; word - ***clean heart***)
  - ◊ *Gold or yellow* (with a picture of heaven, made for all people who accept Jesus Christ as their Savior; word - ***heaven***)
- One piece of meter-long string

Creation

cheating lying Sin

Jesus

clean heart

Heaven

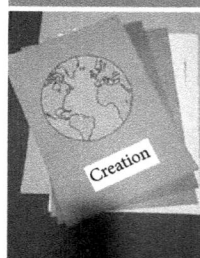

Creation

Steps:

a. Ask the following to the child that you are sharing the gospel with: "Have you ever taken the vision test? It's free, doesn't hurt, and requires only a few minutes."

b. Then, use the string to measure one meter from where the child is to where you will be holding up the graphics on the cardboard; and then start the eye exam.

c. Start by showing them the green "World" card and ask: "What color is this?" When the child responds, it is important to encourage him by saying: "Right, very good; You have very good eyesight!" In case he answers incorrectly, help him by repeating the correct name of the color. Remember that the goal is to teach him the gospel of Jesus. Then continue the dialogue in this way: "And what is this a picture of? (Answer: the world) Right! Now can you read the word that's here? (Answer: creation) Excellent! Did you know that God created the world, and loves everyone, including you, very much?

d. The same sequence of questions applies to the other four visual aids, asking for the color, the word, and then explain a little about the gospel:

- Gray (stained heart; words: sin, lying, cheating, etc). The Bible says that each of us has done bad things. Another word for those bad things is "sin." Sin makes our heart dirty and makes God very sad.

- Red (cross that represents the death of Christ; word: Jesus). Explain how God sent Jesus to suffer and die on the cross for our sins.

- White (clean, white heart; phrase: clean heart); Explain how Jesus wants to forgive us for the bad things that we have done, and give us a clean heart.

- Gold or yellow (heaven; word: heaven). Everyone who has a clean heart because they have been forgiven by Jesus will go to heaven someday to be with Jesus.

e. After the above, say: "Your eyesight is very good, but because of the bad things you have done, your heart is dirty, right? Would you like to ask Jesus to forgive you and clean your heart right now? If so, I am glad to help you." Lead the child in a sincere prayer of faith like the following: "Lord Jesus, I'm sorry for the bad things I have done and I ask You to forgive me. Please give me a clean heart to live like you want me to live, and one day, to be able to go to heaven to be with you forever."

f. After the prayer, congratulate the child on their decision and take note of their personal details (name, address, telephone number, age, etc.). If the child's parents are Christians, be sure to have the child tell them. And within 24 hours of their conversion, contact them to encourage them and set a time to start their first discipleship lesson (Lesson 1, Friends of Jesus, available at www.SdmiResources.MesoamericaRegion.org)

2. "Dialog with bookmarks"

Materials:

- Bible
- Visual aids: five bookmarks with pictures according to the verse and truth to be taught.
  ◊ Bookmark with a heart
  ◊ Bookmark with a sad face
  ◊ Bookmark with a cross
  ◊ Bookmark with a white cloud
  ◊ Bookmark with a happy face

Steps:

Encourage the beginning of the conversation by showing the bookmarks. Then present the evangelistic message as follows:

a. Showing the bookmark that has a heart, explain like this: "God loves you and He wants you to live happily ever after" (John 3:16). You can paraphrase the verse by substituting the expressions "world" and "everyone" for the name of the boy or girl.

b. Then present the second bookmark that has a sad face, and say, "But you cannot be happy and live forever because of sin." Read Romans 3:23, and paraphrase, substituting the child's name for the word "all"; also explain that to sin is to disobey God by doing bad things such as telling lies, cheating on a test, stealing, etc. You can let the child help you add more examples of sin.

c. Third, show the bookmark that has a cross and explain: "You alone cannot do anything to make things better with God; but, Jesus died on a cross a long time ago so that He can take away your sin and bring you closer to God if you ask him to, just as he did for me." Read Romans 5:8 and explain how Jesus died for him or her on a cross, and that with His blood He can clean them of those sins or bad things that do not allow them to be close to God.

d. Then present the bookmark that has a white cloud and make the invitation to repentance and to receive Jesus as their Savior. In this part, you can say: "Your heart keeps all the bad things that you have done during your life so far. God, who sees you, knows you, and loves you, wants you to be different. If you want, you can ask for forgiveness (tell Him you are sorry) for your sins. Jesus already gave his life for you. Right now, He can cleanse you of all that sin and leave your life clean and precious like this white cloud." Read 1 John 1: 9, and ask, "Do you want to do this? If so, I can help you." If they say yes, lead the child in a prayer of confession of their sins and asking Jesus to come into their heart.

e. Fourth, show the bookmark that has a happy face. Assure the child that since they invited Jesus into their heart, He is already there. From then on, Jesus will always be with them. Paraphrasing Revelation 3:20, you can say: "I, Jesus, am knocking at the door of your life and your heart. If you listen to my voice and open the door of your heart, I will come in to you and dine with you; that is to say that we will be together. You invited Jesus in, so you can be sure that He came in and now is in your heart."

f. Lastly, tell the child very gently and emphatically that they can start living differently. For this to be possible, they need to read and study the Bible to learn more about their new friend Jesus. They need to pray asking God for his help every day to do better at home and at school. They also need to attend church activities to meet more Christians and grow in their relationship with the family of God. And, it's important to share with others that God sent Jesus to save the world. (Now begin discipleship lessons with them, starting with Lesson 1, Friends of Jesus, available for free download at: www.SdmiResources.MesoamericaRegion.org)

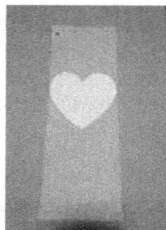

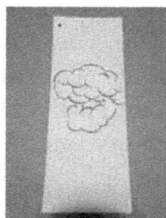

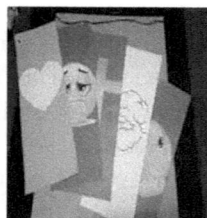

3. "The Five Truths of the Hand"

Materials:

- Bible
- A visual aid of a hand. (This is optional; this method can be applied using one's own hand)

Steps:

There are five truths to show, starting with the thumb and ending with the little finger, making use of the following biblical support:

1. Thumb ("I am a sinner"). Paraphrase Romans 6:23 like this: "We have all sinned, that includes you and me. Sin is everything that God does not like; it is disobedience."

2. Index ("God loves me"). Paraphrase Romans 5:8 like this: "Despite being sinners, God loves us and sent his Son Jesus Christ to save us from sin."

3. Middle ("Christ died for me"). Paraphrase Romans 5:8 thus: "Jesus Christ saves us from sin because when he came to this world, he died on a cross for you and me."

4. Ring/fourth ("I must believe in Him"). Paraphrase Romans 3: 22,24 as follows: "If you believe in Jesus, the Son of God, and trust that He can save you from your sins, then you can be his friend and go to heaven with Him. This is free, you just have to believe." At that time, the child should be asked if they trust Jesus, and if they want to ask for forgiveness. If their answer is yes, lead them in prayer; And if their answer is negative, don't hesitate or be discouraged. Remember that the transforming work is of God, and we are his instruments.

5. Pinky ("I am saved"). Paraphrase Romans 6:23 thus: "Now, you are saved from the death of sin, and the gift that God gives us in Jesus Christ is eternal life with Him." He will be with us always.

(Have the child start lesson 1 of Friends of Jesus as soon as possible.)

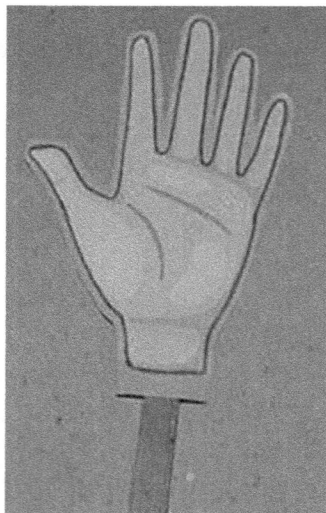
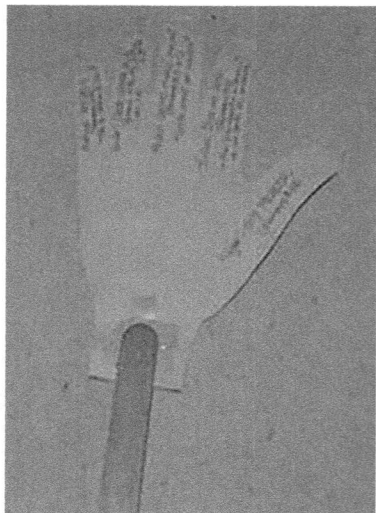

4. "The Wordless Book"

Yellow (or gold) page

Bible passage	John 3:16
Main Point	God loves us and has a place for us.
What is taught with this page	• God is the Creator. • He loves everyone. • God has promised a place in heaven for all who love him. • He is holy.
How to explain this truth to children	Explain that God made all things: plants, animals, rivers, and all people. God loves us very much; and he is preparing a place for his sons and daughters in heaven. He is holy, pure; and so is his home.
Key phrase	But there is one thing that will not enter heaven: sin.

Grey page

Bible passage	Romans 3:23
Main Point	Sin
What is taught with this page	• Concept of sin (bad actions) • Separation from God as a consequence of sin
How to explain this truth to children	Sin is any action that does not please God; that is to say, a bad action. Example: lying, stealing, disobeying parents, insulting others, etc. The Bible says that we must be punished for our sins. This punishment is being separated from God forever (ask the child if he or she admits to being a sinner).
Key phrase	God has a wonderful plan so that you and I don't have to be punished by God for our sins.

Red page

Bible passage	1 Corinthians 15:3-4
Main Point	The person and work of Jesus Christ
What is taught with this page	• Jesus is the son of God. • He took our punishment. • Jesus gave his life for us. • He died; and then he was resurrected.
How to explain this truth to children	Jesus, the Son of God, never did anything wrong. He willingly took your punishment on the cross. God put our sins on Him. Jesus gave His life for us, but he did not stay dead, for he came back to life (he rose again).
Key phrase	Thanks to what Jesus did for us, we can be forgiven.

White Page

Bible passage	John 1:12, Hebrews 13:5b, 1 John 1:9
Main Point	The person and work of Jesus
What is taught with this page	• Invitation to receive Jesus as Savior • Assurance of salvation • Confession of sin
How to explain this truth to children	Read and explain John 1:12. Review by asking questions. Guide the child to pray to receive Jesus as their Savior, and give them the assurance that they are a son or daughter of God, and that He will never leave them. Explain about the confession of sin.
Key phrase	And now that we are children of God, He wants us to know Him better.

Green Page

Bible passage	1 Thessalonians 3:12
Main Point	Growth
What is taught with this page	The child can know God better through the following: 1. Prayer 2. Reading the Bible 3. Attendance at church services, Sunday School classes, etc. 4. Sharing their testimony with other people
How to explain this truth to children	The green color reminds us of the growth of living things, like plants. Explain that now that they have believed in Jesus, they need to grow in Him. To grow, it is necessary for them to pray, read the Bible, attend church, and share the love of God with others. Finally, pray for the child and give them the *Friends of Jesus Bible Study* to start as soon as possible. If they don't have a Bible, help them get one. Finally, record their personal data to follow up with them: name, address, phone number, parents' e-mail, and age. Make sure their parents know what's going on.
Ending	Sincerely and cheerfully congratulate the child on their very important decision.

5. "The ABC's of Salvation"

A dmit you have sinned.

Tell God what you have done, be sorry for it, and be willing to quit sinning.

Romans 3:23—"All have sinned and fall short of the glory of God."

1 John 1:9—"If we confess our sins, he is faithful and just and will forgive us our sins and purify us from all unrighteousness."

B elieve God loves you and sent His Son, Jesus, to save you from your sins.

Ask for and receive the forgiveness God is offering you.

John 3:16—"God so loved the world that he gave his one and only Son, that whoever believes in him shall not perish but have eternal life."

C laim Jesus as your Savior.

Tell what God has done for you.

Love God and follow Jesus.

John 1:12—"To all who received him, to those who believed in his name, he gave the right to become children of God."

Romans 10:13—"Everyone who calls on the name of the Lord will be saved."

D. Resources and / or strategies for mass evangelism

Mass evangelism is one that is directed at a group of boys and girls who can be of different ages. For this type of evangelism to be effective, the principles of creativity and dynamism must be considered, as well as three important aspects: preparations ahead of time, the evangelistic activity, and the follow-up care of the new converts.

Among the mass strategic events for the presentation of the gospel are the following:

• ***Showing The Story of Jesus for children movie***. This well known activity consists of the projection of the children's version of the classic film Jesus, entitled: "The Story of Jesus for children." The projection is usually carried out in an open public place in which the film is projected on a giant screen, preferably for an entire audience of children. The duration of this film is a little over one hour.

• ***Children's evangelistic campaign***. This evangelistic activity is also quite well known. It consists of the presentation of the message of the Good News of salvation to a large group of boys and girls. The program consists of active songs, special presentations and the exposition of the gospel through the use of puppets, mime, theater, drama, preaching, etc. This type of event usually has a motto like "All for Christ," etc., and takes place in a large public place (sports field, stadium, park, etc.).

• ***Happy hour***. This evangelistic event has long been used in various countries to present the gospel to a smaller group of boys and girls. The program begins with a dynamic icebreaker. It continues with active songs, simultaneous games by age, the exposition of the evangelistic message through a class, and ends with a snack. This activity is a good evangelistic option to start working with children living in "white fields" (places where a church has not yet been planted or the gospel preached). The duration of this event is one hour, as its name indicates, and it is suggested to be done in a closed and spacious environment (garage of a house, large room, communal premises, etc.).

• ***Children's evangelistic show.*** This activity has elements of the evangelistic campaign and happy hour. It takes place in a public spacious place, and is aimed at a large group of boys and girls. The program for this contains praise, choreography, contests and the exposition of the Word of God. It also usually has some special presentations, and a snack at the end of the event. What differentiates the children's evangelistic show from the other strategies mentioned is that it is carried out taking advantage of special celebrations such as Christmas, Children's Day, etc. when children are celebrated. So a special date is used to preach the gospel to the boys and girls.

E. Considerations for a Mass Evangelism Event

Recommendations for a successful children's evangelistic event are as follows:

1. Have a team of three to six people (depending on the number of children expected) well trained to work with boys and girls.

2. Involve the boys and girls who regularly attend the church activities by asking them to pray for other children and inviting them to the activity. Also ask the adults, parents and young members of the church to get involved and participate. To do this, you can give them cards on which the boys and girls have written, with the help of their parents, the names of other children, school friends, relatives, etc. for whom they can pray concerning the event.

3. Choose a place to hold the evangelistic event. This can be the patio or garage of a home, a park, a plaza, a field, etc.

4. Plan, organize, and prepare well the entire evangelistic event program well in advance.

5. Develop an effective advertising promotion. For this, you can use flyers (to deliver house to house, at the schools in the area, etc.), posters (to post in businesses), etc. You can also have a parade with the members of the work team, people from the church, and boys and girls from the church, in which the activity is announced.

6. Have a home and leaders available to start a cell group/discipleship class after the evangelistic event, and thus begin discipling the newly converted boys and girls.

F. Preparation of the Children's Event Work Team

Before any mass evangelistic children's event, it is necessary to have the children's ministry in full swing, inside and outside the local church. The evangelistic event is neither the beginning nor the end of this ministry, but an integral part of it, like the rest of the activities that are planned.

An important aspect that should not be overlooked is the planning, organization and development of the scheduled activity. By virtue of this, the following recommendations are provided:

1. Assemble the work team in advance in order to train and prepare them. This takes days, weeks and even months of investment of time.

2. Pray constantly for team members and for the needs and proposed goals of the local church's children's ministry.

3. Analyze the kind of activity to be carried out: an evangelistic campaign, projection of the movie "The story of Jesus for children", happy hour, etc.

4. Decide on the theme of the evangelistic event.

5. Choose the day, place and total duration of the evangelistic event, considering the preparations (preparation of the venue, location and responsibilities of the members of the work team, necessary logistics, location and jobs of helpers, etc.), and the program (it should not last beyond the planned time, and it should be dynamic and participatory).

G. Model of a program for a children's evangelistic event

The realization of an evangelistic event aimed at boys and girls should include the realization of three well-defined parts:

1. Start. This concerns what will be done prior to the beginning of the evangelistic program. Usually it starts 30 minutes before the start of the event. It involves: recorded or live music while the children arrive; ushers at the doors to help the children know where to go; other things happening to set the mood before the activity starts, etc.

2. Development. This is the execution of the evangelistic program itself. It contains everything planned as part of the activity program. Keep in mind that if you are going to show a film, you must consider the duration of the film.

3. Closing. It is the end of the event. During this time, the snack will be distributed to the children attending the event. (If there is enough for the attending parents, they can also be invited.) There should be an invitation to come to the children's discipleship cell/ class, among other matters. About 30 minutes is suggested for this part.

In order to better exemplify the three parts, we present below an illustrative table.

PARTS OF THE EVANGELISTIC EVENT	ACTIVITY DETAILS
Start (Approximately 30 minutes)	• Promotion of the event, and announcements about its start. • Carrying out a game or icebreaker for all the boys and girls who arrive before the start of the event. It is also suggested that leaders meet and socialize with the attending parents.
Development (Approximately 60 minutes)	• Welcome • Active songs • Teaching the evangelistic message through mimes, clowns, puppets, drama, etc. • Simple and clear invitation to receive Christ as Savior and Lord. If time is an issue, the boys and girls who wish to receive Jesus can be asked to just stand up or raise their hands in their respective places. • Small group prayer with the boys and girls who made the decision to accept Jesus. Write down the personal data of those who gave their lives to the Lord. • Praise time • Final prayer
Closing (Approximately 30 minutes)	• Snack • Invitation to discipleship cell/class meetings • Goodbye

H. The Big Brother/Big Sister Plan

Discipleship is an essential ingredient for the success of a children's evangelistic event. The work team will be the ones who will pray for the boys and girls before the evangelistic event, and will visit them at least twice prior to the activity if possible. For the execution of this plan, consider involving the boys and girls who regularly attend church. Some of them may already be ready to be big brothers or sisters. In addition, their help is often decisive in the advancement of discipleship among the children.

After the event is held, the team of children's ministry leaders must commit to weekly visits to the newly converted boys and girls. These visits will have a threefold purpose: to cement God's love by cultivating friendship and communication with the boys and girls who received Jesus as their Savior; encourage them to attend cells/classes and church; and motivate them to join the children's ministry at church. In advance, remember to preview the location for the discipleship meetings. This can be a room, a plaza, a community or municipal center, a garage, etc. It is suggested to find out and / or manage the respective permissions if necessary in order to avoid inconvenience as much as possible.

05 After Evangelism: Discipling Children

Before ascending to heaven, our Lord Jesus said: "Therefore go and make disciples of all nations, baptizing them in the name of the Father and of the Son and of the Holy Spirit, and teaching them to obey everything I have commanded you. And surely I am with you always, to the very end of the age" (Matthew 28:19-20). This disciple-making task applies to all age groups: children, adolescents, youth, adults, etc. Consequently, we must make disciples among boys and girls.

A. After the conversion

Boys and girls who have received Jesus Christ as their personal Savior need the immediate guidance and counsel of mature Christians. Those who do not receive follow-up after such a momentous decision often drift away from the initial commitment they made. Therefore, it is important that the local church's children's ministry team anticipate this complementary and continuing aspect of child evangelism.

Child discipleship is part of the children's ministry. And it can only be carried out effectively by developing a planned, organized and prepared calendar with a series of varied, interesting and practical activities. Likewise, it is necessary to consider various aspects so that the discipleship of newly converted boys and girls after an evangelistic event may bear fruit. We will mention these considerations next.

In light of the previous, the following recommendations are mentioned:

1. Inform the pastor about the new converts. He or she may want to talk to the children to affirm their decision and answer any questions posed. For this purpose, give the pastor a list with the personal data of the newly converted. Invite him/her to accompany the big brother/big sister or disciplers when they make their first visits with the new believers.

2. If possible, begin the follow-up by accompanying the boys and girls as they inform their parents of their decision for Christ. This is particularly important for those from non-Christian households. Allow parents to ask you questions. Some might think that their son or daughter has joined as a member of a church. Assure them that their relationship with the church has not changed; rather, it is their relationship with God which is different. Use this opportunity to give the parents some Christian literature that explains the meaning of salvation.

3. In the first discipleship meetings, affirm the child's decision. Sometimes they may have a hard time understanding that they are already saved, especially in the following cases:

   • When they expected a very emotional response, but did not experience it.

   • When they expected to see dramatic changes in their daily behavior, and did not notice them.

   • When they equate being a Christian with an emotion of "feeling saved" or always being happy.

   • When they receive criticism from adults for normal behaviors for their age.

4. Make a commitment to contribute to the spiritual growth of new believer boys and girls. Help them with the following:

   • To understand what happened at the time of their conversion.

- To appreciate the blessings and resources available to Christians.
- To deal with the doubts, fears and temptations that they will face later.
- To develop a more intimate relationship with God.
- To live the Christian life.
- To value the fellowship of other Christian boys and girls in church.

B. Preservation of the results

Any evangelistic strategy requires a ministry of fruit preservation, otherwise known as discipleship. Winning boys and girls to Christ is just the beginning of ministry to children in the local church, for the complement of it is a discipleship program that lasts indefinitely.

Although it is gloriously true that newly converted boys and girls are exalted to the position of sons and daughters of God, with all the rights and privileges that this entails, we cannot expect them to immediately attain full maturity in the Christian life. In real experience, newly converted boys and girls are babies in Christ, and must grow in grace until they reach the state of spiritual adulthood and beyond.

Analogous to the physical birth of a baby, at the time of being born again, boys and girls should receive tender loving care, as well as patient understanding. They should also be fed the sincere milk of God's Word (simple biblical truths) until they can take stronger food. The children's ministry leaders of the local church, and all brothers and sisters, should nurture new believers and encourage them patiently and lovingly.

Don't instantly look for or expect the little new believer to have a completely sinless life. He or she may continue to disobey, get angry or selfish, and they certainly will! The truth is that although they have truly been saved, they are still in possession of their former nature. The same principles apply to the Christian child and to the Christian adult in dealing with sin, for in both cases, we must help them give their sinful actions to the Lord in sincere confession (1 John 1: 9). In this way, new believers will be able to experience divine forgiveness and cleansing.

Instruct them to continually use the means of grace, such as Bible study, prayer, gathering together, etc. Parallel to this, work on child mentoring, testimony, encouragement, and challenge. Before long, there will be satisfying signs of the Lord's presence in the child's life.

Above all, pray deeply and continually for each one you are discipling. Nothing will ever take the place of intercessory prayer for new disciples. Remember that as a big brother/big sister or discipler, you will become the spiritual father or mother or older sibling of newly believing boys and girls. Study in the Bible how the apostle Paul discipled Timothy, and follow the example of this apostle as you have been called to impact the lives of the Lord's new disciples.

Don't underestimate the value of boys and girls. The conversion of an adult is not more important than that of a boy or a girl. The tendency in many congregations is to think that it is just a boy or a girl. Actually, their salvation is truly glorious. But this is just the beginning. The Christian life begins there, and it spreads more and more. There is still so much for them to learn, experience, and do. How good is our God to put it this way! You will see something new happen progressively in the life of the new believer.

C. Basic teachings for the initial discipleship of newly converted boys and girls

We must help the children in their knowledge and growth as disciples of the Lord Jesus. For this, the teaching of the following topics is suggested: God, Christ, the Bible, the church, the Christian community, and the knowledge of the reality of other children in other countries. Of these general concepts, only those aspects that are within the reach of the mental capacity of boys and girls based on their age should be taught. The list that follows will give you an idea of what the believing child can understand in relation to biblical teaching. (A great resource to help teach all of these topics is Friends of Jesus, available for free download at: www.SdmiResources.MesoamericaRegion.org)

GOD	• He is our Father who is in heaven, and He loves us. • He is the Creator of all things. • He is our protector who protects us from the dangers to which we are exposed. This protection is given to us through our parents and other people. • He provides for our needs. • He is our helper when we're sad, giving us the answers to our problems. • Disobeying God is sin.
JESUS	• He is the Son of God. • He was born and raised as a child, and was obedient to his parents. • He died for the sins of all people (children, youth, adults, etc). • He came back to life, went to heaven, and he wants to be in our life and heart. • He loves boys and girls, and is their friend. • He is preparing a home in heaven for those who love him. • He has the same power that God has, since Jesus is God.
THE BIBLE	• It is the Word of God. • It tells us what the Lord wants us to know and do. We must love, respect and obey it. Bible stories are true; they are not fairy tales.
THE CHURCH	• It is the house of God, and we must love it, take care of it, and respect it. • We can invite other boys and girls to the church. We learn about God in his home.

D. Recommendations for discipling children

The following are recommendations that we suggest you take into account when discipling children. They will help you in the conservation of the fruit harvested after the children's evangelistic event.

1. With the members of the children's ministry team from your local church, plan everything regarding the discipleship of new converts: day or days of meetings of the discipleship cell or class, meeting place, disciplers, discipleship materials to use, activities to do, among others.

2. Develop a calendar of scheduled activities inside and outside the meeting place or church, taking into consideration the boys and girls as main participants.

3. Hold regular meetings with the entire children's ministry team from your local church for the purpose of planning, organizing, preparing and evaluating all activities. The weekly meeting serves as the brain of the work to be done: it controls the functions, activities and coordinates everything.

4. Make all activities for boys and girls interesting, creative and well planned, including Bible classes, children's services, etc.

5. Bear in mind that the care and attention that should be given to the newly converted is similar to that given by a shepherd to his sheep, or that of a hen to her chicks. That is to say, it must satisfy all their needs. Some live in extreme poverty, which causes them to not eat properly, or attend church.

6. Help each new believer to be sure that they are now a son or daughter of God after their decision to receive Jesus Christ as their Savior and Lord.

7. Design a system to record attendance at cell meetings/class sessions in such a way that disciplers can identify the "sheep" who are absent from any children's activities subsequent to the evangelistic event. This will help the big brothers/big sisters to be aware of what is going on with the little new believers.

8. Guide and / or teach biblically so that believers can overcome sins, dangers and problems.

9. Teach new disciples to set aside time each day for personal devotions. The means of grace are extremely vital. Find a way of providing them with a Bible (preferably one for children if they are very young) if their parents cannot afford one.

The child must learn that they need to pray and read the Bible every day. If they cannot read yet, you can suggest that their parents read it to them. The believing child should also be encouraged to meet regularly with those who have the same faith as them. Sunday school and children's worship are great for this. It is encouraging for them to know that there are other boys and girls who love the Lord too.

10. Discipleship can have a special class during Sunday school or worship hours. But above all, remember that this work goes beyond the classes taught in a space or place since it is a transfer of life; hence the importance of paying attention to the little ones in faith, such as the genuine care that a mother or father has for their children.

E. Responsibilities of the big brother / big sister or discipler

Once the child has accepted Christ, he or she should be assigned to a big brother/big sister (mature believer) or discipler who is committed to praying daily for him or her and helping them grow into Christlikeness.

Keep in mind that what our younger siblings in faith need most is a Christian friend, someone who cares about them, that is, a sincere person to advise and help them in their spiritual life. So establishing trust is one of the key factors. Pray to God that this will flow naturally and gradually increase.

During each weekly activity, the main mission is to confirm and affirm the child's faith in Jesus Christ. At each meeting, the big brother/sister should develop friendship and trust with the child, help them with any difficulties, answer any questions, encourage them to have their daily devotions, encourage them to attend the various children's ministry activities, and witness to their friends and relatives. Also remember that every meeting and / or visit should end with prayer.

Finally, the discipler must greet them warmly wherever they see the believing boy or girl: in the market, on the street, etc. They must show them that this friendship is permanent and unconditional, and does not only happen during cell meetings/discipleship class, etc.

F. Suggestions for using the movie "The Story of Jesus for Children" in children's ministry

The Story of Jesus for Children is a tool that can be very useful if we know how to use it fully. We talked a bit about this resource during the section on mass evangelism, but it should be noted that this tool can also be used in other areas of the spiritual formation of boys and girls. In children's ministry, we have different ministries or programs, among which the film in question can be very useful. For example, during the Vacation Bible School (VBS), we can discuss the life of Jesus in one week. During the weekly Bible classes, we can spend 15 minutes a day watching the film, arriving at the end of the movie at the end of the week. In Children's Church, we can talk about the life of Jesus for a month by spending 15 minutes watching parts of the film on Sundays. At a children's camp, we can divide the time and watch part of the movie each night instead of, or as part of, a sermon.

In Sunday school classes, the film can be shared during classes in December, or in the month that the resurrection of our Lord is celebrated, or at a time that is deemed best.

Each of these activities can end with a call to salvation, and thus apply evangelism to the different ministries or programs of SDMI (Sunday School and Discipleship Ministries).

BONUS

Plan of Salvation

To guide a child to Christ, it is necessary to be clear enough so that he or she can understand it. We must use age appropriate language. For example, instead of talking to them about sin, we must clearly tell them what this means (lying, deception, theft, bad language, etc.). We must also find the best time and not make an evangelistic call in every class. For this reason, the message on the last day can be evangelistic. If we have a private time with the child in which we can bring this up, we must not miss the opportunity. The four points to remember when leading a child to Christ are:

1. I acknowledge that I have done bad things that do not please God.

2. I feel bad about them and want to stop doing them.

3. Please forgive me Lord and accept me as your child.

4. I believe that you have forgiven me.

To help you in this process you can use the following model:

(Additional methods can be found in the section of Evangelistic Methods for Personal Evangelism starting on page 29.)

③ Please forgive me, Lord, and accept me as your child.

② I feel bad for that and I want to stop doing those things.

④ I believe that you have forgiven me!

① I know that I have done bad things that don't please God.

Instructions:

1. Photocopy this page.
2. Cut along the dotted line.
3. Fold in four as shown on the previous page.

www.ingramcontent.com/pod-product-compliance
Lightning Source LLC
Chambersburg PA
CBHW060624030426
42337CB00018B/3179